Unveiling the Enigmatic Beauty of Switzerland.

MONTREUX, SWITZERLAND TRAVEL GUIDE 2024

ETHAN BRISBANE

TABLE OF CONTENTS

CHAPTER 1
INTRODUCTION
1.1 Overview Of Montreux
    a. An Imaginative Tapestry:
    1.2 Why 2024 and Montreux?
        a. The Magic of Montreux Remains:
    1.3 A Brief History Of Montreux

CHAPTER II
PLANNING YOUR TRIP
    2.1 Best time to visit
    2.2 How to Get to Montreux
    2.3 Entry and Visa Requirements

CHAPTER III
ACCOMMODATIONS
    3.1 Best Hotels in Montreux
    3.2 Budget-Friendly Options
    3.3 Special Places to Stay

    CHAPTER IV
EXPLORING MONTREUX
    4.1 Must-Visit Attractions
    4.2 Hidden Gems
    4.3 Outside Activities

CHAPTER V

DINING AND CUISINE

    5.1 Regional Swiss Delights

    5.2 Restaurants with Fine Dining

CHAPTER VI

NIGHTLIFE AND ENTERTAINMENT IN MONTREUX

    6.1 Highlights of the Montreux Jazz Festival

    6.2 Bars and Nightclubs

    6.3 Cultural Fusion in Nightlife:

    6.4 2024 Cultural Events

CHAPTER VII

PRACTICAL INFORMATION

    7.2 Safety Advice

    7.3 Medical Services

CHAPTER VIII

FREQUENTLY ASKED QUESTIONS

    8.2 Are there any particular cultural customs or protocols to be mindful of?

    8.3 What are some tips for getting the most out of the Montreux Jazz Festival?

    8.4 What COVID-19 criteria will be in effect in Montreux in 2024?

CHAPTER IX

UPDATED 2024 INFORMATION

    9.1 Calendar of Events and Festivals

9.2 Modifications to Local Laws
9.3 Novel Features or Advancements

CHAPTER X
LANGUAGE AND COMMUNICATION
10.1 Frequently Used French Phrases
10.2 Practical Translations for Vacationer

CHATRER XI
CONCLUSION
11.2 The Next Stages of Your Travels

CHAPTER 1

INTRODUCTION

1.1 Overview Of Montreux

Welcome to Montreux, a hidden jewel perched on the shores of Lake Geneva, where the Alps meet the entrancing waters in a delicate manner, providing a sanctuary for those seeking adventure as well as peace of mind. By 2024, Montreux will be remembered as a timeless location that skillfully combines a rich past with a contemporary charm.

a. An Imaginative Tapestry:

Envision a village where colourful flower-lined promenades intersect cobblestone streets. With its stunning backdrop of snow-capped mountains and Belle Époque architecture, Montreux beckons you to enter a picture-perfect environment. Photographers' dream and travellers' utopia, every corner tells a tale, and every view is a work of art.

Happy

1.2 Why 2024 and Montreux?

a. The Magic of Montreux Remains:

Music enthusiasts have always found refuge in Montreux, and this year is no different in 2024. With the prestigious Montreux Jazz Festival taking centre stage this year, there's promise of an even more captivating encounter. The festival transforms into an inspiring celebration of music and culture thanks to its diverse lineup of international performers and its picturesque lakeside location.

b. Accepting the Symphony of Nature:

Montreux welcomes nature lovers with broad arms in 2024. The majestic Swiss Alps provide a haven for nature lovers, with everything from tranquil boat trips on Lake Geneva to hiking paths that lead to expansive views. The beautiful surroundings of Montreux invite you to explore and re-establish a connection with nature; they are more than just a picturesque backdrop.

c. Cultural Treasures Revealed:

Beyond its picturesque scenery, Montreux is known for its diverse cultural heritage. Explore the History of Chillon Castle, a marvel of the Middle Ages that carries ghosts of the past. Visit the Chaplin's World Museum to learn about Charlie Chaplin's legacy, or visit the charming Lavaux Vineyards to learn about Swiss winemaking. Montreux is a voyage through time and culture, not just a place to visit.

1.3 A Brief History Of Montreux

a. The Melting Pot of Languages:

You'll hear a symphony of languages in Montreux as French, German, and Italian blend together to represent the multicultural identity of Switzerland. If you don't speak the language well, don't worry; people will welcome you with open arms, and a simple "Bonjour" will go a long way.

b. Montreux Signature Dish :

Savour the gastronomic treats that Montreux has to offer; fondue is a local favourite. Easy yet delicious:

melted Swiss cheese paired with crispy bread. You're in for a culinary treat if you pair it with some regional wine.

C. Montreux's Ever-changing Weather:

The weather in Montreux is as varied as the scenery. 2024 is going to be a great year for strolls by the lake, but don't forget to bring a light jacket for the cool mountain breezes. The unpredictable weather lends a thrilling element to your trip to Montreux.

d. Getting Around with Swiss Precision:

The effective public transportation system in Switzerland makes navigating Montreux a breeze. The travel is just as enjoyable as the destination, whether it's a leisurely boat excursion or a picturesque rail ride.

e. Timeless Elegance Meets Modern Comfort:

Montreux provides a variety of lodging alternatives, ranging from opulent hotels with lake views to little boutique motels. All of them provide not only comfort but also a full immersion in the distinct atmosphere of the town.

This is but a taste of what 2024 will bring to Montreux. Please don't hesitate to contact me if you need more information or would like to explore any particular area in more detail!

CHAPTER II

PLANNING YOUR TRIP

2.1 Best time to visit

Selecting the ideal season to visit Montreux is essential to fully appreciate its varied allure. The ideal time to go will depend on your interests, as this Swiss gem is enhanced by the changing of the seasons.

a. Springtime (March to May)
With a flash of colour, Montreux comes alive as the snow starts to melt. Springtime brings a riot of flowers to the promenades beside the lake and the nearby Lavaux vineyards. It's the perfect season for leisurely walks and visiting cultural attractions without the summer throng because of the mild temperatures

b. Summertime, from June to August:

The summer months are thrilling times to visit, especially in July when the world-famous Montreux Jazz Festival takes centre stage. Warm weather invites you to take Lake Geneva boat trips or go hiking and other outdoor sports in the Alps. The dynamic energy of fellow travellers, along with music and events, bring the town to life.

c. Fall (September through November):

Montreux embraces a more understated beauty as the leaves turn golden. For those looking for peace, autumn offers a more personal experience. You can enjoy the beauty of the changing seasons because the weather is still comfortable. Wine lovers should take advantage of this wonderful opportunity to visit the Lavaux Vineyards.

c. Winter, (December to February):

Montreux turns into a snow-covered winter paradise, encircled by peaks covered in snow. Although there isn't much snow in the town itself, ski resorts nearby entice those who love the snow. It is a pleasant and enchanted winter destination because of the Christmas markets and festive lights, which give the environment a magical touch.

2.2 How to Get to Montreux

a. By Air

About ninety kilometres away, Geneva Airport (GVA) is the closest major airport. It's simple to travel to Montreux from the airport by car, rail, or shuttle service. An additional alternative is Zurich Airport (ZRH), which requires a little more time to get to by train—roughly three hours.

b. Via Train:

Train travel in Switzerland is known for being both economical and picturesque, and this is also the case in Montreux. Enjoy breathtaking vistas of Lake Geneva and the Alps during the approximately one-hour train ride from Geneva to Montreux. Travellers will find the Montreux train station useful due to its central location.

c. Via Automobile:

If you would rather have more freedom when driving, Montreux has excellent road connections. You may take your time exploring the breathtaking scenery during the scenic drive, which departs from Geneva and takes around 1.5 hours. Major airports provide rental automobile services.

d. By Watercraft:

Consider going on a boat tour of Lake Geneva for an arrival that is unforgettable. Although it's not the most traditional way to get around, it provides a relaxing and beautiful way to go to Montreux so you can enjoy the scenery and the beauty of the lakefront.

2.3 Entry and Visa Requirements

Due to Switzerland's membership in the Schengen Area, short-term visa-free travel to many other countries is now easier for travellers. You must verify the particular prerequisites according to your nationality. Make sure that the expiration date on your passport is at least three months in advance of when you intend to depart.

a. Schengen Area Visa:

You'll need to apply for a Schengen Visa if you're not from a nation where visas are not required. With this visa, you can spend up to 90 days in the Schengen Area within 180 days. Apply as far ahead of time as possible for your intended trip.

b. Travel Guard:

Although not necessary for obtaining a visa, travel insurance is strongly advised. It offers protection against unforeseen circumstances including lost property, medical problems, and cancelled trips. If you intend to participate in winter sports, find out if your insurance covers things like skiing.

2.4 Money and Financial Concerns

a. The Swiss Franc (CHF):

The Swiss Franc is the accepted form of payment in Montreux (CHF). Although credit cards are generally accepted, it's a good idea to have extra cash on hand, particularly for local businesses or markets. There are plenty of ATMs in Montreux where you may easily withdraw cash.

b. Rates of Exchange:

Prices in Switzerland can be somewhat higher than in other European nations, despite the country's reputation for having a good level of living. Keep up with the latest exchange rates so that you can plan your budget with knowledge. Banks and exchange offices offer currency exchange services.

c. Changing Cultural Attitudes:

Tipping is not required in Switzerland, however, it is customary. Although restaurant invoices frequently include service charges, it is nice to round up or leave a modest gratuity. It's customary to tip housekeeping in hotels.

d. Planning a Budget:

There are many different lodging options in Montreux, ranging from opulent hotels to more affordable options. The cost of dining can vary, but there are often tasty and reasonably priced options to be found by visiting the neighbourhood markets and bakeries. When creating your budget, take into account the things you want to do, such as going to festivals, going on outdoor adventures, or sampling the local food.

With this thorough information, you should be well on your way to organising your trip to Montreux. Please don't hesitate to contact me if you have any specific inquiries or if you want to learn more!

CHAPTER III

ACCOMMODATIONS

3.1 Best Hotels in Montreux

a. Fairmont Le Montreux Palace:

The Fairmont Le Montreux Palace is a shining example of luxury and grace, tucked away on the banks of Lake Geneva. With its magnificent Belle Époque architecture, this renowned hotel provides a royal experience together with amazing views of the Alps and the lake. Savour fine dining at its restaurants, unwind in luxurious accommodations, and revitalise yourself at the spa. Immersed in the magnificence of Montreux, the Fairmont Le Montreux Palace is more than just a hotel. It's an opulent refuge.

b. Majestic Grand Hotel Suisse:

Located in the centre of Montreux, the Grand Hotel Suisse Majestic offers a unique combination of contemporary amenities and traditional charm. This four-star hotel, which has a lake view, is conveniently located in the middle of the town's attractions. The hotel's patio has expansive views of Lake Geneva, and the rooms are elegantly furnished. Situated close to the Montreux Jazz Festival and offering gracious hospitality, the Grand Hotel Suisse Majestic ensures that your stay will be unforgettable.

c. The Royal Plaza Hotel & Spa in Montreux:

The Hotel Royal Plaza Montreux & Spa is a fantastic option for anyone looking for an opulent getaway with a dash of modern elegance. With its cutting-edge amenities and contemporary style, this hotel is a comfortable haven. The spa's amenities, which include a wellness centre and indoor pool, offer a peaceful retreat. Convenience and elegance are combined at Hotel Royal Plaza Montreux & Spa, which is conveniently located near Lake Geneva and the town centre.

3.2 Budget-Friendly Options

a. Accommodation Bon Rivage:

Affordability without sacrificing charm is what Hostellerie Bon Rivage offers. This hidden treasure offers breathtaking views at a fraction of the price and is situated along the lakeside promenade. The welcoming staff gives a personal touch to your stay, and the accommodations are basic yet cosy. Due to its convenient location near the Montreux Music & Convention Center and ease of access to public transportation, Hostellerie Bon Rivage is a great option for tourists on a tight budget.

b. Helvetie Hotel:

The charming and reasonably priced Hotel Helvetie has a rich history that dates back to the late 1800s. This reasonably priced hotel is perfectly situated in the centre of Montreux, making it easy to walk around the town. Cosy rooms with a distinct touch are provided by the hotel's historic charm. Stay at Hotel Helvetia and have a nice experience without going over budget.

c. Youth Hostel Montreux:

The lively and dynamic Montreux Youth Hostel is ideal for budget-conscious but daring travellers. This hostel, which has individual rooms and dorm-style accommodations, looks out over Lake Geneva. The common areas promote conversation among visitors, fostering a lively and welcoming atmosphere. Backpackers and those looking for a social experience will find Montreux Youth Hostel to be an excellent option due to its affordable rates and breathtaking views.

3.3 Special Places to Stay

a. Le Mirador Spa & Resort:

Situated atop Mont Pèlerin, with a breathtaking view of Lake Geneva and the Alps, Le Mirador Resort & Spa provides an unparalleled lodging experience. This five-star resort offers a getaway from the busy town core by fusing luxury and peace. The wellness amenities, which include an infinity pool, enhance the luxurious experience, while the roomy rooms and suites offer expansive vistas. Le Mirador Resort & Spa is a haven for people looking for a quiet and secluded getaway, not merely a hotel.

b. Hotel & Jazz Café Montreux:

Enjoy a musical immersion at the Montreux Jazz Café & Hotel. This hotel honours the town's musical heritage and is housed inside the Montreux Jazz Festival structure. Every chamber has a different theme honouring jazz greats and the history of the festival. The rooftop terrace's breathtaking view of Lake Geneva combines well with the ambient sounds. The Montreux Jazz Café & Hotel is a symphony of flair and culture for music lovers.

c. A Conventional Swiss Chalet Stay:

Staying in a typical Swiss chalet will give you a true Alpine experience. Charming chalets with wooden interiors and views of the mountains may be found in Montreux and the neighbouring districts. Immerse yourself in the alpine atmosphere while enjoying a rustic yet comfortable stay at these quaint lodgings. A stay in a Swiss chalet, whether it's tucked away in the mountains or with a view of the lake, brings a little piece of the past to your Montreux vacation.

You can adjust your stay in Montreux to fit your preferences and price range with the help of our guide. Montreux is waiting for you, whether you want luxury, affordable options, or something different. Please let me know if you have any specific requests or if you would like more information!

CHAPTER IV

EXPLORING MONTREUX

4.1 Must-Visit Attractions

a. Chillon Mansion:

Nestled on the shores of Lake Geneva, Chillon Castle is a historical gem that will take you back to mediaeval times. This 12th-century stronghold is characterised by its  stone walls and turreted turrets. You'll discover stories about knights, prisoners, and the strategic significance of the castle as you meander through the maze-like passageways and chambers. With its romantic lakeside setting, Chillon Castle is a quintessential representation of Montreux's illustrious past.

b.Montreux Jazz Festival

At the renowned Montreux Jazz Festival, experience the beat of Montreux. Every July, the town is transformed into a worldwide platform for legendary performers of jazz,  blues, and rock music during this musical spectacle. The passionate music of worldwide musicians fills the shores of Lake Geneva, creating an exhilarating atmosphere. The Montreux Jazz Festival offers a unique experience at the nexus of culture and melody, regardless of your level of musical appreciation.

c. The Rochers-de-Naye

Reach new heights on the peak of Rochers-de-Naye, a mountain reachable by picturesque cogwheel train. As you reach the summit, take in the expansive views of

Lake Geneva and the surrounding Alps. Rochers-de-Naye is a wildlife sanctuary as well as a viewpoint. See these cute animals in their natural environment by going to the marmot park. The Alpine Garden provides an

adventurous look at the region's distinctive flora. A trip through the heart of Montreux's natural splendour is Rochers-de-Naye.

4.2 Hidden Gems

a. Lavaux Vineyards

Set off on a journey through wine at Lavaux Vineyards, a UNESCO World Heritage Site tucked away among the hillsides with a stunning view of Lake Geneva. This undiscovered jewel is a patchwork of quaint villages, terraced vineyards, and stunning lake views. Take a bike ride or on foot over the vine-covered slopes, stopping at local vineyards to sample fine Swiss wines. Lavaux

Vineyards provides a flavour of the region's viticultural legacy and is a hidden gem for wine lovers.

b. The World of Charlie Chaplin

Visit Chaplin's World to enter the whimsical world of the renowned silent cinema performer Charlie Chaplin. A memorial to Chaplin's life and film legacy, the museum is situated in the neighbouring town of Corsier-sur-Vevey. Take a tour of Chaplin's former home, Manoir de Ban, and discover interactive displays including his movies and personal belongings. Chaplin's World is a fantastic voyage through the humour and inventiveness of a cinematic classic, not merely a museum.

c. The Glion Institute of Advanced Learning

Discover the Glion Institute of Higher Education's educational allure in Montreux. This esteemed hospitality management school is perched on hills above the town and provides stunning views of Lake Geneva. Take a guided tour to discover the beautiful surroundings and architecture of the campus. Glion Institute of Higher Education elevates your Montreux itinerary, whether you're thinking about a career in hospitality or just enjoying intellectual quality.

4.3 Outside Activities

a. Hiking Trails

Take a hike along one of the beautiful trails in Montreux. The area welcomes hikers of all skill levels, from strenuous mountain hikes to tranquil lakeside strolls. The Lakeside Promenade encourages you to stroll through the town at your speed, while the Rochers-de-Naye trail provides a picturesque climb. Explore the various landscapes of Montreux and find hidden waterfalls, alpine meadows, and beautiful views.

b. Aquatic Sports

Enjoy the cool embrace of Lake Geneva while participating in a range of water activities. Take a leisurely boat ride or go kayaking or paddle boarding along the pristine waters to see Montreux from a different angle. The beaches around the lake offer a peaceful environment for a swim or a lazy afternoon in the sun. In Montreux, water sports provide the ideal balance of action and leisure.

c. In the Alps, skiing

Scream with excitement as you ski in the breathtaking Swiss Alps, which are only a short drive from Montreux. World-class slopes are available for skiers of all skill levels at the neighbouring resorts of Verbier, Gstaad, and Villars. The snowy alpine scenery and powder make for an exciting winter wonderland for both novice and experienced skiers. Relax in comfortable mountain chalets and savour Swiss après-ski customs after a day of skiing.

This introduction to the sights, hidden treasures, and outdoor pursuits of Montreux is only the start of your adventure. Discover Montreux's rich tapestry, whether you're drawn to the natural beauty of the Alps, enthralled with history, or both. Please don't hesitate to ask me questions or to request more information about any certain topic!

CHAPTER V

DINING AND CUISINE

5.1 Regional Swiss Delights

a. Fondue:

Enjoy fondue for the ultimate Swiss dining experience. With the help of long forks, diners gather around a communal pot of melted cheese to enjoy this classic delicacy. Gruyère and Emmental cheeses combine to make a thick, creamy combination that is tasty and cosy. Fondue is a must-try culinary tradition in Montreux, whether it's consumed in a quaint bistro by the lake or a rustic mountain lodge.

b. Raclette:

Savour the deliciousness of raclette, another traditional dish from Switzerland. This dish consists of pickles, cured meats, and cooked potatoes with melted Raclette cheese scraped straight on top. The contrast of flavours and textures creates a filling and substantial supper. Savour this delicious Alpine treat in the friendly setting of a Raclette supper with friends and family.

c. Rösti:

The simplicity of Rösti, a Swiss potato dish that personifies comfort food, will delight your taste buds. Grated potatoes make a delicious base for a variety of toppings when they are pan-fried till brown and crispy. Rösti exemplifies the skill of transforming common materials into a delectable dish, whether it is served as a side dish with a substantial meal or coupled with smoked salmon for breakfast.

d. Swiss Chocolate:

Satisfy your sweet craving with the renowned chocolate from Switzerland. Due to its proximity to well-known chocolate-producing regions, Montreux has an extensive selection of delicious artisanal chocolates. Every taste, from smooth truffles to bars of Swiss chocolate, celebrates the nation's mastery of chocolate-making. Discover the smoothness of Swiss chocolate and indulge in local chocolatiers.

5.2 Restaurants with Fine Dining

a. Le Montreux Palace:

At Le Montreux Palace, fine dining meets luxurious surroundings for a gourmet adventure. This Michelin-starred fine dining restaurant is located within the renowned Montreux Palace Hotel. Renowned chefs have crafted a cuisine that features a blend of international and Swiss flavours. Savour a harmonious blend of flavour and presentation in a classy atmosphere with a view of Lake Geneva.

b. Restaurant de l'Hôtel de Ville:

In the neighbouring Crissier, the Michelin-starred Restaurant de l'Hôtel de Ville is the perfect place to learn the art of good dining. This restaurant, which is well-known for its superb food, takes diners on a culinary tour through French and Swiss traditions. A great dining experience is promised by the creatively and precisely created seasonal cuisine. Food connoisseurs will find it to be a destination due to its charming, intimate atmosphere.

c. Le Deck:

At Le Deck, enjoy fine dining while taking in views of the lake. This restaurant, which is housed in the Fairmont Le Montreux Palace, mixes exquisite food with breathtaking scenery. With a focus on local, fresh ingredients, the menu blends Mediterranean and Swiss elements. Enjoy a gourmet feast at Le Deck while dining on the patio with sweeping views of Lake Geneva.

5.3 Quaint bakeries and cafes

a. Jazz Café Montreux:

Experience Montreux's musical atmosphere at the Montreux Jazz Café. For those who enjoy coffee, this café, housed in the Montreux Jazz Festival complex, provides a comfortable haven. Jazz greats are honoured by the colourful décor, which also creates a distinctive and lively environment. At the Montreux Jazz Café, savour handcrafted coffee, delectable pastries, and the upbeat energy of jazz music.

b. Le Cygne Café:

Café du Cygne has the allure of a classic Swiss café. This cosy café is tucked away in the centre of Montreux and radiates nostalgia. A refuge of calm is revealed to guests with the scent of freshly brewed coffee and the enticement of handcrafted pastries. Café du Cygne embodies the spirit of Montreux's café culture, whether you're taking a leisurely afternoon tea or drinking espresso at the bar.

c. Au Chat Noir:

Relax in the laid-back vibe of Au Chat Noir, a small café that captures the essence of Montreux's creative scene. This café is a gathering place for both locals and tourists, with its colourful paintings and retro décor. Savour handcrafted pastries, fragrant teas, and a varied menu that will satisfy everyone's palate. Au Chat Noir invites you to stay, converse, and enjoy the spirit of creativity that characterises Montreux.

The culinary scene in Montreux presents a delicious blend of local specialties, global inspirations, and a hint of musical magic. Enjoy a feast for the senses in

Montreux, whether you're indulging in Michelin-starred luxury or Alpine classics. Please don't hesitate to ask me questions or to request more information about any certain topic!

CHAPTER VI

NIGHTLIFE AND ENTERTAINMENT IN MONTREUX

This is the lively world of Montreux's nightlife and entertainment, where the town's cultural pulse bursts to life as the sun goes down. Montreux invites you to experience a variety of entertainment possibilities in 2024, ranging from the internationally known Montreux Jazz Festival to intimate nightclubs and cultural events.

6.1 Highlights of the Montreux Jazz Festival

A Symphony of Jazz, Blues, and Beyond

Overview: The highlight of Montreux's entertainment offering is the Montreux Jazz Festival, which attracts tourists from all over the world. Since its founding in 1967, this venerable festival has developed into a celebration of many musical genres, such as techno, jazz, blues, and rock.

Highlights:

1. International Headliners: The event has a reputation for drawing in well-known performers. The roster, which features both modern stars and jazz greats, attests to Montreux's reputation as a global centre of the music industry.

2. Scenic Venues: The festival's choice of locations is one of its distinctive pleasures. Events are held in a variety of locations, including small clubs and outdoor stages with panoramic views of the Alps and Lake Geneva.

3. A Variety of Genres: While jazz is at the centre of the festival, its scope has broadened to accommodate a spectrum of musical styles. Rock fans, electronic music fans, and lovers of the blues may all find something to enjoy in the varied program.

4. Night Jam Sessions: The late-night jam sessions during the event are legendary, even outside of the scheduled concerts. An exciting mood is often created when musicians from various bands gather together for spontaneous concerts.

5. Cultural Fusion: With artists from a variety of backgrounds, the festival highlights Montreux's multiculturalism. The musical experience gains a distinct depth from this mix of civilizations.

ADVICE FOR FEST-GOERS:

- **Make a Plan:** The festival takes place over several days, with several events taking place at once. Arrange your plan ahead of time so you can see your favourite performers as well as new ones.

- **Explore Beyond the Main Stage:** Even while the main artists are worth seeing, check out smaller locations for more personal shows and unanticipated musical experiences.

- **Appreciate the Lakeside Ambience:** Take a stroll along the Lakeside Promenade during intermissions. A mystical atmosphere is created by the sound of music and the tranquil lakeside location.

- **Participate in Workshops and Talks:** Participate in seminars and discussions with artists to enhance your experience. Learn about the origins of the music and the tales that inspire it.

6.2 Bars and Nightclubs

Where the Night Comes to Life

Overview: Beyond the festival, Montreux has a vibrant nightlife with a wide variety of bars and nightclubs to suit all preferences. Montreux offers something for everyone, whether your preference is for a sultry cocktail lounge or a bustling dance floor.

Nightclubs:

1. Claude's Funky Bar: Inspired by the great Claude Nobs, who founded the Montreux Jazz Festival, this bar honours the history of music in the area. Savour specialty cocktails, a lively atmosphere, and live music.

2. Amnesia Club: A popular option for people looking for a lively dance floor is Amnesia Club. It's the place to go for a night of dancing, with regular DJs spinning a blend of mainstream and electronic favourites.

3. Miles Davis Hall: Despite being well-known for its festival contributions, Miles Davis Hall occasionally changes into a nightclub. Take in the arena in a whole new way with the vibrant throng and throbbing beats.

Bars:

1. Harry's Bar: Welcome to Harry's Bar, a traditional cocktail lounge with an elegant atmosphere that will never go out of style. Savour a well-made cocktail as you take in the retro vibe and maybe listen to some light jazz.

2. The Funky Claude's Bar: Apart from its vibrant nightlife, Funky Claude's Bar provides a comfortable ambiance for individuals wishing to relax. Enjoy a beverage, strike up a discussion, and take in the unique décor.

3. Jazz Café Montreux: Live jazz concerts are available at Jazz Café Montreux, a casual venue that offers the ideal fusion of music and cocktails. For those looking for a more laid-back evening, it's a cosy atmosphere.

6.3 Cultural Fusion in Nightlife:

The nightlife of Montreux reflects the city's multiculturalism. International performers are drawn to the town for the festival, but local talent is also highlighted in the pubs and nightclubs, giving up-and-coming musicians a stage on which to perform.

Advice for Nightlife Enthusiasts:

- **Examine Various Locations:** Every bar and nightclub in Montreux has a distinct personality. Discover the variety the area has to offer by checking out a range of locations.

- **View Event Schedules:** Themed evenings and special events are common features of Montreux's nightlife. Examine local listings or event calendars to make sure your visit coincides with noteworthy events.

- **Interact with Residents:** The nightlife in Montreux is a great way to meet people from the area. Engage in conversation, seek out advice, and become involved in the town's social life.

- **Dress Code:** Despite the laid-back vibe of Montreux, certain establishments could have a dress code, particularly when there's live music or other special events. Make sure you're dressed adequately by checking ahead of time.

6.4 2024 Cultural Events

Beyond Music: A Year-Round Cultural Tapestry

Overview: Montreux is not only a summertime getaway for music fans . The town offers a wide variety of events all year long on its rich and varied cultural calendar. Montreux welcomes culture in all its manifestations, from film festivals to art exhibitions.

Highlights:

1. Montreux Comedy Festival: The town is filled with laughter when the Montreux Comedy Festival takes place. Enjoy funny improvisations, comedy acts, and stand-up routines by well-known and up-and-coming comedians.

2. The Film Festival of Montreux: International films are screened as part of the Montreux Film Festival, which honours cinematic brilliance. Film magic is brought to Montreux by the festival, which features both compelling fictional stories and thought-provoking documentaries.

3. Montreux Arts and Culture Center: The Montreux Arts and Culture Center, which opened its doors in 2024, acts as a centre for visual arts, theatre, and other cultural activities. Visit galleries, go to shows, and take in Montreux's vibrant artistic atmosphere.

Year-Round Cultural Engagement:

Montreux is dedicated to fostering cultural interaction that goes beyond one-time events. The community actively supports a strong arts scene, gallery shows, and local artists. Throughout the year, visitors may happen across spontaneous performances, art projects, and cultural programs.

Tips for Cultural Explorers:

- **View Event Schedules:** The cultural activities in Montreux take place all year long. To find out the most recent details on forthcoming cultural events, consult the event calendars and town announcements.

- **Check Out Art Galleries and Cultural Venues:** Investigate the galleries, studios, and cultural venues in your area. The city of Montreux's dedication to the arts is demonstrated by its backing of up-and-coming artists and preservation of its cultural legacy.

- **Attend Conversations and Roundtables:** Talks, panel discussions, and artist Q&A sessions are common cultural events. Come to these workshops to learn about the creative process and have thought-provoking discussions.

- **Take part in workshops:** Cultural workshops provide you the opportunity to get hands-on experience and fully immerse yourself in different art forms. Taking part in these events, such as painting workshops or film discussions, improves your cross-cultural experience.

The Night in Montreux is a canvas that is painted with the sounds of jazz, humour, and visual storytelling. Montreux's entertainment and nightlife promise amazing experiences, whether you're dancing at a jazz-inspired nightclub, sipping drinks in a vintage lounge, or taking in the town's year-round cultural tapestry. Think about the variety of options that await you after dusk as you make your travel plans. Please ask any questions you may have about the Montreux entertainment scene or if you have any unique preferences. Prepare to let your nights be guided by the rhythm of Montreux!

CHAPTER VII

PRACTICAL INFORMATION

Now let's get down to business and discuss how to navigate Montreux safely, smoothly, and with a dash of local knowledge.

7.1 Getting Around Montreux

a. Public Transport:

Make use of Montreux's effective public transit system to start your journey conveniently. Because of its small size, the town is easily explored on foot; however, if you want to go farther or take a more picturesque route, the Montreux public transportation system is available. To get about the town and its environs, take the buses and trains. As a hub, the central rail station connects you to neighbouring cities and points of interest.

b. Boat Cruises on Lake Geneva:

Boat trips on Lake Geneva can infuse your travels with a hint of romanticism. A boat ride on the immaculate waterways offers a distinctive viewpoint of Montreux's lakeside allure. Savour the stunning surroundings while taking leisurely cruises to nearby towns like Lausanne or Vevey. Well-organised boat schedules provide a leisurely and picturesque substitute for conventional modes of transportation.

C. Taxi Services:

When in need, choose the ease of cab services. In Montreux, taxis are widely accessible and provide a pleasant and effective way to get around, particularly for shorter distances or when door-to-door service is preferred. Taxis are available for hailing on the street or at special taxi stands located in strategic areas.

d. Rental Automobiles:

Rent a car and drive around Montreux and its environs at your leisure. There are options for renting cars, giving you the freedom to explore the Swiss Alps or find undiscovered treasures off the usual track. The attractive routes and well-kept roads of Montreux provide for a delightful and picturesque road trip experience.

e. Cycling and strolling:

Savour the laid-back charm of Montreux whether cycling or walking. The town's well-designed bicycle routes and pedestrian-friendly layout allow walking and cycling attractive forms of transit. Ride through the charming vineyards, stroll along the lakefront promenade, or discover the town's charming streets. It is recommended to enjoy the panoramic splendour of Montreux at a leisurely pace.

7.2 Safety Advice

a. Public Protection:

Although Montreux is proud of its reputation as a secure travel destination, it's always important to exercise caution wherever you go. The people of the town are warm and inviting, and the crime rate is kept low. Take the usual safety precautions, such as being alert to your surroundings and keeping a check on your valuables, especially in crowded situations.

b. Being Weather Ready:

Get ready for the variety of weather that Montreux has to offer. The weather can change, with cool winters and pleasant summers. Make sure to pack appropriately, bringing layers in case the weather suddenly changes. To ensure a comfortable and safe experience, check weather forecasts before embarking on outdoor activities or mountain exploration.

c. Safety in the Mountains:

Give mountain safety a top priority when travelling through the Alps. When hiking or skiing, consider your ability level and select terrain or slopes that are appropriate for you. Always have maps, water, and clothing appropriate for the weather with you. For more distant regions, make sure to check the status of the trails and let someone know about your plans.

d. Water Security:

Respect water safety regulations and responsibly enjoy Lake Geneva. When participating in aquatic activities, abide by the swimming areas that have been specified and observe any posted cautions. The temperature and currents in Lake Geneva can change quickly, so be cautious and make sure you know the safety precautions for the water sport you want to participate in.

e. COVID-19 Points to Remember:

Keep yourself updated on any new COVID-19 policies and procedures. The situation may have changed after my last update in 2022. For the most recent information on travel restrictions, mask requirements, and vaccine needs, check with your local government and health agencies. Make sure you have all the required paperwork and follow all health and safety regulations while you are there.

7.3 Medical Services

a. Healthcare Institutions:

You may relax knowing that Montreux offers high-quality healthcare services. The town is equipped with state-of-the-art hospitals and medical facilities, guaranteeing that guests can obtain essential healthcare when needed. Pharmacies are easily accessible for minor medical issues or prescription needs.

b. Travel Guard:

For additional peace of mind, think about getting travel insurance. Although the medical facilities in Montreux are first-rate, having travel insurance protects against unplanned medical costs, missed flights, and emergencies. If you intend to participate in outdoor activities like hiking or skiing, make sure your insurance covers them.

c. Services for Emergencies:

Get acquainted with the emergency contact details. Know the emergency numbers for the local authorities and ambulance services in case of any medical or safety problems. The security of its citizens and guests is of utmost importance to Montreux, and when help is needed, it arrives quickly.

d. Wellness and Pharmacies:

Locate pharmacies for your well-being and medical needs. Montreux pharmacies provide a variety of over-the-counter drugs, personal hygiene goods, and wellness items. Helpful pharmacists are on hand to answer any questions you may have about health.

With these useful suggestions, navigating Montreux becomes a pleasurable and worry-free experience. Montreux extends a warm welcome to you and is dedicated to your safety and well-being, whether you're taking in the local cuisine, touring the Alps, or just strolling around its picturesque streets. Please let me know if you have any special queries or if you would like more information!

CHAPTER VIII

FREQUENTLY ASKED QUESTIONS

Let's discuss some often asked questions about Montreux, offering practical advice and pointers for a smooth visit.

Concerning Montreux

8.1 Which kind of transportation works best in Montreux?

With its small size and well-functioning transportation infrastructure, Montreux provides several easy options to get around the town and its beautiful environs.

a. Public Transport:

The public transportation system in Montreux is highly efficient for getting around the city. There are buses and trains in the town, which facilitates convenient transportation. Serving as a hub, the central train station offers connectivity to neighbouring cities and points of interest. In addition to being practical, public transportation provides beautiful vistas of the Swiss countryside.

b. Cycling and strolling:

For a more relaxed investigation, think about going for a walk or a bike ride. It's fun to stroll along the lakeside promenade or explore the lovely districts of Montreux because of its pedestrian-friendly layout and well-marked cycling pathways. You can take your time and enjoy the town's natural beauty while walking and cycling.

c. Taxi Services:

In response, taxis are easily accessible and offer a more individualised door-to-door service. Taxis are a practical option, particularly for shorter trips or when you want a direct and pleasant form of transportation, even though Montreux is reasonably navigable on foot and by public transportation.

d. Lake Geneva Boat Cruises:

Answer: Boat trips on Lake Geneva are a great way to see the town and surrounding surroundings. They offer a unique experience. The immaculate waters present a distinct angle on the lakeside allure of Montreux. Boat cruises make for a fun and romantic form of transportation, whether you're going to nearby cities like Vevey or just taking a leisurely cruise.

8.2 Are there any particular cultural customs or protocols to be mindful of?

Comprehending and honouring the customs and traditions of the region improves your experience in Montreux. Here are some crucial things to remember:

a. Salutations and Terminology:

Since Montreux is a cosmopolitan city, courteous welcomes are greatly appreciated by the residents. The majority language is French, however many locals can also speak English. Saying "Bonjour" or "Merci" (thank you) is a small yet meaningful gesture. Shaking hands with new acquaintances is usual, and being amiable is always valued.

b. Customs Tipping:

In Switzerland, leaving a gratuity is not required, but it is customary. Although restaurant invoices frequently include service charges, it is courteous to round up or leave a modest gratuity. It's customary to tip housekeeping in hotels. Tipping shows gratitude for a job well done.

c. Clothes Code:

The answer is that people in Switzerland are proud of how they look, and they regard tidy clothing as polite. Although Montreux is known for its laid-back vibe, particularly when engaging in outdoor activities, it's a good idea to dress suitably for more formal occasions such as fine dining restaurants or cultural events.

d. Timeliness:

In Swiss culture, being on time is highly regarded. Being punctual is a respectful gesture, whether you're going to a concert or another scheduled event. Allow extra time in your schedule to accommodate for unanticipated delays and transportation.

8.3 What are some tips for getting the most out of the Montreux Jazz Festival?

One of the town's highlights is the Montreux Jazz Festival, which draws visitors from all over the world who love music. Here are some tips for maximising this historic occasion:

a. Make a Plan:

Plan your visit to the event by looking over the schedule. A wide range of musicians from different genres are on the schedule for the Montreux Jazz Festival. Get acquainted with the schedule, taking note of the shows you can't miss. For popular shows, think about getting tickets in advance.

b. Investigate Outside of the Main Stage:

Inquire about different venues for distinctive performances while the main stage has headliners. The Montreux Jazz Festival is not limited to the main stage;

smaller locations provide intimate performances by up-and-coming artists. Don't be afraid to explore several locations for a more varied experience.

c. The atmosphere along the lake:

The answer is to take in the festival vibes beside the lake. The festival is set against the breathtaking backdrop of Montreux's lakefront location. During intermissions, enjoy the local fare, stroll down the promenade, and take in the enchanted atmosphere that the music and landscape create.

d. Participate in talks and workshops:

To learn more about the world of music, take part in seminars and workshops. Renowned musicians frequently conduct masterclasses, debates, and workshops at the Montreux Jazz Festival. Attend these workshops to gain a deeper appreciation for the artwork and develop a closer relationship with the festival.

e. Seize the Moments:

The best response is to carry a camera or smartphone to record the special moments. The Montreux Jazz Festival is a visually striking event. Take notes on your favourite shows, the lively ambiance, and the stunning scenery. Make enduring memories by telling other festival attendees about your experiences.

8.4 What COVID-19 criteria will be in effect in Montreux in 2024?

Perhaps by the time I wrote my last update in 2022, the world had changed. Still, it's important to keep yourself updated on COVID-19 regulations in case you plan to visit Montreux in 2024. Here are a few broad things to think about:

a. Verify Any Travel Restrictions:

Answer: Make sure you are aware of any admission requirements or travel limitations before you book your trip. Remember that depending on where you are from, laws may differ. To make sure you have the most recent information on entrance procedures, visit official government websites and get in touch with the appropriate authorities.

b. Check the safety and health precautions:

Remain up to date on the health and safety protocols that Montreux has put in place. For information on any rules about mask-wearing, social distancing, and cleanliness standards, check with the local government, lodging facilities, and event planners. To protect your safety and the safety of others, be ready to adhere to these regulations.

c. Testing and Vaccination:

Check to see if there are any immunisation or testing requirements. Check if access to specific locations or events requires proof of vaccination or negative test results. Bring the necessary paperwork with you to make your trip more efficient.

d. Keep abreast of Event Development:

The pandemic is changing, so keep up with what's going on, especially with the Montreux Jazz Festival. For the most recent information on updates, modifications, and festival safety procedures, see the official website and local news outlets.

e. Travel Guard:

One option is to look into travel insurance that covers unforeseen cancellations or adjustments. Considering the current dynamic, obtaining travel insurance offers financial security in the event of unanticipated COVID-19-related events. Make sure any potential delays to your travel arrangements are covered by your insurance.

These responses are meant to offer helpful advice on frequently asked topics regarding Montreux. Please do not hesitate to contact me if you have any more questions or require further details on any particular subject!

CHAPTER IX

UPDATED 2024 INFORMATION

9.1 Calendar of Events and Festivals

a. Jazz Festival in Montreux:

Update: In 2024, the Montreux Jazz Festival is still a prominent event in the town's cultural schedule. It continues to draw musicians and music lovers from around the globe as one of the most well-known music festivals in the world. To find out the most recent lineup, timetable, and any special events scheduled for the 2024 edition, visit the official festival website or consult local sources. The event promises a unique musical experience with its signature jazz, blues, and rock blend.

b. The Comedy Festival in Montreux:

Update: 2024 brings more fun to the town thanks to the Montreux Comedy Festival. Comedic performances and stand-up comedians will be included at this event, which highlights humour from different cultures. The Montreux Comedy Festival presents a wide range of comic talent in an engaging and friendly environment, perfect for anyone who enjoys comedy or is just seeking for a fun night out.

c. Festival du Film de Montreux:

Update: The celebration of creative cinema will go on at the Montreux Film Festival. This festival presents a range of films, from fictional narratives to documentaries, and gives a platform to up-and-coming filmmakers. To learn about upcoming screenings, panel discussions, and chances to interact with the film industry, consult the festival schedule. Captivating storytelling and visual beauty are added to the town's cultural tapestry by the Montreux Film Festival.

9.2 Modifications to Local Laws

a. COVID-19 Indicators:

Update: Montreux continues to be dedicated to the safety and health of the public. Visitor expectations on adherence to health guidelines should not change, while exact measures may change depending on the scenario worldwide. For information on any current COVID-19 rules, such as those about mask use, social distancing, and admission restrictions, check with your local authorities. The safety and enjoyment of residents and visitors is of utmost importance to Montreux.

b. Initiatives for Sustainable Tourism:

Update: Montreux continues to take steps to promote sustainability. The town still places a high priority on environmentally friendly activities, such as encouraging responsible tourism and reducing waste. It is advised of visitors to support these initiatives by being aware of how they affect the environment. Investigate environmentally beneficial modes of transportation, take part in neighbourhood conservation initiatives, and support Montreux's dedication to sustainable tourism.

c. Attempts at Cultural Preservation:
Update: Montreux is still committed to protecting its rich cultural history. In 2024, there will still be initiatives to preserve historical landmarks, honour regional customs, and honour the town's creative heritage. It is recommended that visitors participate in cultural activities, go to local gatherings, and lend assistance to projects aimed at preserving Montreux's distinctive character.

9.3 Novel Features or Advancements

a. Center for Arts and Culture in Montreux:
Update: Visit the Montreux Arts and Culture Center to immerse yourself in a creative hotspot. This centre, which opened its doors in 2024, acts as a hub for cultural events, performances, and visual arts. The Montreux Arts and Culture Center, which has galleries, studios, and an adaptable event area, is intended to promote and develop regional and global artistic talent.

b. Renovations to the Lakeside Promenade:

Update: Thanks to recent promenade upgrades, enjoy a better lakefront experience. The famous Lakeside Promenade in Montreux has been renovated to create an even cosier setting. The promenade has been upgraded with seating places, vegetation, and lighting to add to its appeal and make it a wonderful place for strolls along Lake Geneva's shore.

c .Expansion of Experiences in Cooking:

Update: As dining alternatives increase, try out new gastronomic pleasures. The gastronomic landscape of Montreux is constantly changing, with new eateries and cafés providing a variety of culinary delights. Visitors can enjoy a variety of cuisines that showcase the town's culinary innovation, from cutting-edge fine dining places to intimate cafes with distinctive concepts.

d. Alpine Wellness Retreat in Montreux:

Enjoy a restorative stay at the Montreux Alpine Wellness Retreat. This brand-new spa resort offers a tranquil getaway in the neighbouring Alpine region.

With spa services, yoga classes, and wellness programs available, this nature-lodged retreat lets guests relax and revitalise while taking in the spectacular views of the Swiss Alps.

In 2024, Montreux is expected to offer a diverse range of cultural activities, improved experiences, and a persistent dedication to sustainability. Discover the appeal of this lakeside treasure in Montreux, whether you're drawn to it for world-class music festivals, thrilled about new cultural endeavours, or keen to learn about the most recent advancements. Please let me know if you have any special queries or if you would like more information!

CHAPTER X

LANGUAGE AND COMMUNICATION

10.1 Frequently Used French Phrases

a. Salutations and Simple Expressions

- **Bonjour** - Good morning / Hello
- **Bonsoir** - Good evening
- **Salut !** - Hi! / Hello!
- **Comment ça va ?** - How are you?
- **Bien, merci ! Et toi ?** - Well, thank you! And you?

b. Politeness and Gratitude

- **Merci** - Thank you
- **Merci beaucoup** - Thank you very much
- **S'il vous plaît** - Please

- **Excusez-moi** - Excuse me
- **Pardon** - Sorry / Pardon me

c. Asking for Assistance

- **Où est la gare ?** - Where is the train station?
- **Pouvez-vous m'aider ?** - Can you help me?
- **Je suis perdu(e)** - I am lost
- **Parlez-vous anglais ?** - Do you speak English?
- **Je ne parle pas bien français** - I don't speak French well

d. Ordering Food and Drinks

- **La carte, s'il vous plaît** - The menu, please
- **L'addition, s'il vous plaît** - The bill, please
- **Je voudrais un café, s'il vous plaît** - I would like a coffee, please
- **L'eau minérale, s'il vous plaît** - Mineral water, please
- **C'est délicieux !** - It's delicious!

e. Numbers

- **Un, deux, trois, quatre, cinq** - One, two, three, four, five
- **Dix, vingt, trente, quarante, cinquante** - Ten, twenty, thirty, forty, fifty
- **Cent** - Hundred
- **Mille** - Thousand
- **Combien ça coûte ?** - How much does it cost?

f. Language Advice for Visitors
Acquire Basic Words:

Though many people in the area understand English, it can still be more enjoyable if you know a few simple French words. Salutations, appreciation, and let's hope this helps establish some connections. Even if your French is not very good, the locals will nonetheless appreciate the attempt.

a. Make Use of Civil Expressions
Advice: French society places great importance on politeness. Saying "Excusez-moi" when asking for help,

"Bonjour" while entering a store or restaurant, and "Merci" when expressing thanks all help to foster a pleasant exchange.

b. Have patience and be honest.
Advice: When overcoming language obstacles, it's important to be open and patient. If you come across someone who doesn't speak English well, attempt to communicate with them in plain terms and be patient. The majority of locals will be gracious in return and appreciate the effort.

c. Work on Your Pronunciation
Advice: Gaining confidence might come from practising fundamental pronunciation. Pay attention to how frequent sentences sound. Speaking with native speakers and repeating words might make you feel more at ease when speaking French, as the pronunciation of the language can vary.

d. Make Use of Language Apps:
Advice: For speedy translations, think about utilising language applications. Phrase translation and sign

interpretation can be aided by programs such as Duolingo, Google Translate, or local language apps. It can be useful to have these instruments on hand, particularly in more isolated locations.

10.2 Practical Translations for Vacationer

a. Directions and Transportation

- **Où est la gare routière ?** - Where is the bus station?
- **Je voudrais un billet pour Genève, s'il vous plaît** - I would like a ticket to Geneva, please
- **Combien de temps pour aller à Vevey en train ?** - How long does it take to go to Vevey by train?
- **Où est l'arrêt de taxi le plus proche ?** - Where is the nearest taxi stand?
- **Je voudrais louer une voiture pour la journée** - I would like to rent a car for the day

b. Accommodation

- **Où est l'hôtel [Nom de l'hôtel] ?** - Where is [Hotel Name]?
- **Est-ce que le petit déjeuner est inclus ?** - Is breakfast included?
- **Puis-je avoir une chambre non-fumeur ?** - Can I have a non-smoking room?
- **Quelle est l'heure de départ ?** - What is the check-out time?
- **La clé de ma chambre, s'il vous plaît** - The key to my room, please

c. Dining

- **Je voudrais réserver une table pour deux à 20 heures** - I would like to book a table for two at 8 p.m.
- **Avez-vous un menu végétarien ?** - Do you have a vegetarian menu?
- **L'addition, s'il vous plaît** - The bill, please
- **C'est délicieux !** - It's delicious!
- **Puis-je avoir l'assaisonnement à part ?** - Can I have the dressing on the side?

d. Emergency Situations

- **Où est l'hôpital le plus proche ?** - Where is the nearest hospital?
- **Appelez une ambulance, s'il vous plaît** - Call an ambulance, please
- **J'ai perdu mon passeport** - I have lost my passport
- **Pouvez-vous m'aider ?** J'ai besoin d'aide médicale - Can you help me? I need medical assistance
- **Où est le commissariat de police ?** - Where is the police station?

Knowing a few basic words in French will help you have an even more delightful time navigating Montreux. Whether you're placing an order at a restaurant, requesting directions, or expressing your gratitude, speaking the local tongue makes your trip more enjoyable. Please let me know if you have any special queries or if you would like more information!

CHATRER XI

CONCLUSION

Thank you for finishing your virtual tour of Montreux! We have thoroughly investigated the quaint town situated on the banks of Lake Geneva, revealing its many cultural offerings, breathtaking scenery, and exciting events. Let's review our journey's highlights and plan the next stages for your real-life excursion as we come to an end in Montreux.

11.1 Summary of the Experience in Montreux

a. A Musical and Cultural Symphony:

The world-famous Montreux Jazz Festival and other cultural events like the Montreux Comedy Festival and Montreux Film Festival demonstrate how Montreux's heart beats to the beat of music. The town's lakeside location makes for a peaceful backdrop that combines humour, music, and cinematic creativity to create a unique experience.

b. Gorgeous Scenery at Every Turn:

The expansive vistas of the neighbouring Alps and Lake Geneva are a magnificent delight for the eyes. Every corner of Montreux, from the Lakeside Promenade to the summit of Rochers-de-Naye, reveals a different captivating landscape. Experiences like exploring the mediaeval Chillon Castle, taking in the breathtaking views of the Lavaux Vineyards, and taking in Charlie Chaplin's artistic legacy are all like brushstrokes on the beautiful canvas that is Montreux.

c. Gourmet Treats and enchanting cafes:

The cuisine of Montreux takes you on a gourmet voyage with Swiss specialties like raclette and fondue. The town's restaurants offer a taste of both tradition and innovation, ranging from elegant restaurants with views of Lake Geneva to small cafes with a strong local flavour. Savour regional wines, indulge in Swiss chocolate, and let the aroma of freshly brewed coffee lead you as you explore Montreux's culinary delights.

d. Multicultural Amity and Kindness:

A cosmopolitan paradise, Montreux extends a warm welcome to guests. A true sense of welcome is fostered by the town's dedication to sustainable and responsible tourism, as well as the warmth and eagerness of the residents to share their language and culture. Get involved in the local community and pick up a few French words, and you'll discover that Montreux is an embracing of culture rather than just a place to visit.

11.2 The Next Stages of Your Travels

As you conclude your virtual tour, think about the next actions you should take to get to Montreux in person.

a. Making Travel Plans:

Select the Appropriate Time

Advice: Choose the time of your visit according to your tastes. Winters provide skiers with a wintry paradise, while summers are colourful with festivals and outdoor pursuits. Montreux is shown in all its transitional splendour in the spring and fall, which offer a balance.

b. Accommodations and Transportation:

A tip is to look into your possibilities for lodging and make reservations well in advance. Plan your travel arrangements, taking into account your preference for either the flexibility of a leased automobile or the ease of public transportation. Choose from a variety of lodging options in Montreux, including quaint guesthouses and opulent hotels, depending on your tastes and price range.

**c. Take Part in Cultural Events
(Participate in Local Events):**

Advice: Verify the festival schedule to see when you can visit. Plan your visit around the Montreux Jazz Festival or other cultural happenings, if at all possible. These celebrations enhance your experience by drawing you into the lively cultural scene of the community.

d. Investigate Hidden Treasures:

Take a detour from the usual route. Though famous sights are a must-see, don't miss discovering Montreux's lesser-known treasures. To find the genuine appeal of the town, visit nearby art galleries, take a stroll through less-known neighbourhoods, and interact with the locals.

e. Take in the Beauty of Nature (Outdoor Excursions):

Advice: Bring appropriate gear for outdoor activities. Make sure you have the appropriate equipment whether you're skiing in the winter or taking part in water activities on Lake Geneva, hiking in the Alps, or both. The natural beauty of Montreux entices investigation, and enjoying these outdoor activities is enhanced when you are well-prepared.

f. Calm beside the Lake:

Advice: Savour the peace of the lakeside. Enjoy boat rides, wander along the Lakeside Promenade at your leisure, and soak in Lake Geneva's tranquillity. These times provide a serene counterpoint to the lively energy of the town.

g. Explore Culinary Wonders in More Depth:
regional tastes

Try some of the regional Swiss specialties. Go beyond raclette and fondue and try some local favourites. Talk to locals to learn about hidden restaurants, sample various wines, and let your taste sensations lead you around the varied culinary scene of Montreux.

h. Experiences with Cultural Dining:
Advice: For a more engaging meal, try dining at nearby restaurants. Look for eateries where the community congregates, enjoys street cuisine, and participates in traditional mealtime rituals. This opens your eyes to Montreux's social attitude and expands your culinary horizons as well.

i. Make Friends with Locals
(Etiquette in Language and Culture):
Advice: Keep studying and using fundamental French phrases. Speaking with locals in their tongue helps to establish a stronger bond. Being aware of cultural customs, such as courteous salutations and thank-you

notes, improves communication and makes a good first impression.

j. Participate in Local Workshops:

Advice: Take part in events and workshops in your community. Attending a language exchange program, traditional art lesson, or culinary class is just one of the many ways to meet locals, exchange stories, and get a better sense of life in Montreux.

k. Accept the Unexpected:

Advice: Be receptive to coincidental discoveries. With its abundant natural beauty and rich cultural heritage, Montreux never fails to astound its guests. Give yourself permission to stray from your schedule, trust your gut, and enjoy the unplanned experiences that are what make a trip unique.

Finally, Montreux entices a melodic array of experiences, ranging from the tranquil beauty of Lake Geneva to the soul-stirring songs of the Montreux Jazz Festival. As you organise your trip, keep in mind that Montreux is an invitation to fully immerse yourself in a tapestry of natural beauty, culture, and gastronomic delights rather than merely a place to visit. Good luck and have fun on your way to Montreux! Please get in touch if you need help or have any more queries. Happy travels!

Printed in Great Britain
by Amazon